LOVE

LETTERS

TO

THE

WORLD

∼ love letters to the world ∼

MEIA GEDDES

◎ Poetose Press

ISBN 978-1-945366-88-8 (paperback)

ISBN 978-1-945366-12-3 (e-book)

Library of Congress Control Number: 2016941897

Published by Poetose Press

Printed in the United States of America

First Edition

Cover by Sara Zieve Miller

CONTENTS

—✦—

~ I ~

To fall into you

My dear world,

There is something sunny and blue about you. I would like to embrace blue, sometimes, but it can be difficult to embrace a color. I would like to slide through the blue and let it become gray and let it wash away. I would like to fall into you, a raindrop hitting earth, for if you are a raindrop hitting earth, you become the world. I think to be the soaking sphere of a raindrop is a very good thing, for you evaporate time and again, then always rediscover yourself as something else and also the same. Perhaps I am just a slip of space to you, world, but that is okay. Here I am, bits of slips of space. I wonder — how to explain — it's like when it rains and all the pitter-patters seem to accumulate someplace other than the ground, someplace terribly close to the toes or the eyes or the heart. That is how I hope we can be — pouring into one another in different ways.

With love,
M

My dear world,

Sometimes I wonder if I taste the air of you enough. You are a very airy being and a hard one to taste. I suppose the way I want to go about meeting you is the way I want to go about being, just a bit at a time. One cannot fill the pages of life as with a lined notebook. This is it — to kiss a sphere of air, to sketch and spread things out as in a book of blank pages, the logic haphazard, the moments of a life scattered in bright flashes of light, scratches of color, space upon space to create subtle shapes. This is what it is to taste the being that is you, to live abundantly. Why is it that a warm wind lets me feel your heart beat just a little more? Your winds can fill a person to the brim if they are not careful, world. And your light, pouring into my hair, into the crevice behind my neck. I like how you can make me feel like the sun, like something close to truth.

With love,
M

My dear world,

Peering across a long expanse of space, full of trees and people and other things weaving in and out and about, one becomes aware of the depths of space and layers of light all around. It is extraordinary how we are present in this particular slice of space or this particular layer of light, and it begins to feel like we are slipping in and out of time. And this is in fact a way of thinking that has sense, for one exists solely in one's own time. Another's particular moment of existence in time will always be imperceptibly different from mine. Perhaps the only exception is when making love. But maybe not even then. Can we exist within a sphere beyond ourselves, our singular existence? Is this what loving is? If we made love, you and I, what could we create? I think I should like to create something gentle.

With love,
M

My dear world,

I lie in my room and the shaking bed above assures me of life. I imagine she knows the color of his eyes in different shades of light. That she can fathom the depth of his displacement at any given time. That, when thinking of him, she is touching him, and seeing him, she is holding him in her eyes. That the tips of her fingers are attuned, beautifully, logically, to the moments of his heart, and that she can detect who he is not even if she never will determine who he is. She has a feeling of him, I am sure, in the tilt of his head, and when she touches him I hope she feels a vague notion she has arrived someplace extraordinarily good. In his company I imagine she loves herself a little less. I hope they feel brought back into the world — to you — making love up there.

With love,
M

My dear world,

Maybe one must be still. I forget to let language sweep me up, let words inhabit my body like song, let myself love. Sometimes there is nothing, nothing to do but love. That is the best kind of thing that stillness can breed. Also the kind of thing that makes you wonder how many folks have wanted to be a tree, that makes you recall a good kiss or how the moonbeams seemed to have slipped under your feet and how you wanted to fall into the sky. I wonder if the greater the number of minutes one dwells on kisses past, the greater one extends life. Sitting still, I feel the immensity of life at the tips of my toes, and it occurs to me that one of the most important investments one can make is in the matter of shoes — how one dresses one's feet for the world. Practicing living through sitting, I find myself ready to rise.

With love,
M

My dear world,

A circle is a thing of unity and boundaries. I am wary of circles for I like things that resist perfection and separation, like curving lines and smudged ink. Yet I want to live in spiraling spheres, to embrace the recurring moment. We are creatures of a circling nature. Always returning, somehow, to ourselves, to others, to you, whether we wish it or not. Ever circuitously curving about our lives. Do circles hold a kind of instinctive truth? I think I shall go out to buy a clock with hands sometime soon. After all, I am not familiar with anyone who lives a linear life. Maybe a life is simply a circle. Maybe a life is simply a little kiss, a little circular kiss. Can one kiss you? If one could kiss the world, it would be a great big circular kiss. Kisses to you.

With love,
M

My dear world,

Do moments leave remnants? Wisps of hair with memories of hands passing through, breaths recalling release. Each moment fills the other moments till all moments become one. Maybe words lengthen a life by slowing it down to moments. The rhythms of breath are moments moving, living slowly. We shall simply live as many moments as we can and bend to our bliss and send our lives to places we have never heard of and be as much as we are, redefining our flight moment to moment, from the remnants of moments. There is a willingness to the page, as there is to life. A quiet being I strive to be, like a moment. Like when it is snowing and raining, the snow pitter-pattering away. It is good to be the pitter-patter of snow, no? To be an unexpected kind of moment in time. I hope we can always offer each other such moments, my dear.

With love,
M

My dear world,

I do not know of a beautiful sentence or a true sentence, the most beautiful, the truest. All I know is that the sentences stream out from varying depths of desire and fear, and that the way one shapes a sentence is not a reflection of the self in one moment, but of the accumulation of many moments, and more precisely, the unsaid, indefinable conception of what lies both within and without the self. And then after you have written a sentence, you think things of it and you have a feeling of who you were, but you never really can know. Just like the way folks can shift into your life and slip into your being without you ever really seeing, except maybe eventually you will feel the imprint of their coming or going and know something good came along even if you did not immediately recognize it for what it was. You gather the real sweetness about a person you once knew and you have a taste of what it means to come home. All of this is to say that I wonder if you will begin to feel like home.

With love,
M

My dear world,

Home is a strangely onomatopoeic word. It offers itself
in a small opening of the mouth, a possibility of existence
in a kind of blessed comfort, a nest of sorts. I wonder if
I can ever really feel at home with you. I walk forward,
always, now, as if I am making my first steps. For there are
always questions — how to live with you being the chief
one, of course. I wonder if one can make one's life into
a series of projects. I wonder if finding a home within
oneself is enough. Someone once told me that if you
offer someone something with a smile, they will more
willingly receive it. I wonder if I smile at you, will you
receive me more easily? I wonder if home is freedom,
and if I find a home in you, I will be free. I wonder if
you are free and how wanting you are.

With love,
M

My dear world,

There was the Lost Generation and the Beat Generation, and so I wonder — what are we? Maybe we are the Time Generation, trying to navigate ourselves to a lost beat. But it is hard to attune ourselves to the moment because we need to know ourselves and we need to know the moment. And yet — I aspire to be like the sky, and I do not believe the sky ever looks across itself and wonders who it is. So let us be here, sitting at the heels of the sun, holding on to something like language. In this vast space what else is there except language to hold? Writing, I am a child sitting on my mother's front lawn, stick in hand, sketching things into the grass. I move back and forth, rocking with the beat of my heart. I try to be myself as much as possible. Maybe all you need to do is find the heartbeat in everything. And if writing is living, the discovery of the beat of a heart, then when you read me, you are living by my side.

With love,
M

My dear world,

I have found that one can always turn to the sentence. Beginning and completing sentences can secure some artificial feelings of success: If one wishes to create, one must have a table and chair of one's own. If one does not know how to end one's tale, one must consider bringing the protagonist to an end. If one wants to know love for certain, one must behold something that makes one so breathless as to feel strangely intense, concentrated, the self in its final encapsulation. If one wants to know how to live, the choreography, the mechanics of it all, one must learn to dance. I await, wondering how we shall proceed. I must admit it feels as though I have begun the sentence and will soon realize you will not be helping me finish it.

With love,
M

My dear world,

We like to consider where we come from, to consider where we are, to consider where we are going. We like to comprehend the precise placement of our selves, our thoughts, whatever it is we are. So I suppose the notion of a person displaced, without agency, is terrifying to a degree. Yet maybe one becomes accustomed to not knowing. That may be why I feel a bit more comfortable with you, world, for from an early age I learned how to live with not knowing. I rejoice in the quiet wholesomeness of your unknowability. After all, we live in movement. Nothing remains the same. The sky, for instance — the sky knows nothing of sameness. It knows of clouds and clouds and clouds, so soft, undulating about. And you know, world, the flavor of softness is so often sweetness. I turn to you even when I do not know it.

With love,
M

My dear world,

I found it endearing to see the woman sitting in a chair with her legs curled up like a fern, for it reminded me of spring. She looked into the distance, and looking at her, I felt I was looking into a dream, like peering into another dimension, like peering into a mystery. I think, world, it is good to be the kind of person who looks into the distance and who looks upon others looking into the distance. The eyes yearn and squeeze forward, and it becomes the most affordable form of placement and displacement a person could seek. The placement of displacement. For sometimes the best form of placement is displacement, as my understanding of displacement is that there will always be a return, when one learns and feels and exists the most, when one comes home to oneself from afar. And sometimes the best form of displacement is placement, when everything seems to be speeding in the still.

With love,
M

My dear world,

Sometimes nothing can be still. The mind and heart wander. I know a man who has a voice of love because every time he speaks it is as if he is saying, "I love you." I know a woman in my head who wants to say, "I love you," but she lives in a world of metaphor. A house filled with light and a voice calling out softly, so softly, "My love?" There is a man who thinks nothing can be his own until he has loved it. Men and women who wonder if they are in love, if they love. There is a woman I know and I wonder how much of her is love. I surrender to the texts of my head and heart. We do not think or live in sentences, but in waves of fragments, sense and non-sense. I realize you do not receive love letters often, my dear, and I think it is because any persons with feelings for you find themselves rather incoherent.

With love,
M

My dear world,

I suppose we must be wary of fragmenting ourselves, but I am content to have become decidedly plotless. There is a thirst for openness in the air, and I have determined to pay attention to the spaces around me, to wonder what happens when spaces intersect. We fear space, I think. I like to twist shapes out of the looming space, but maybe all one can do is plunge forward, madly embracing space. I try for a feeling, a question of sorts, an itch on my soul, a vague daze in a moment or two in time. Sometimes I feel vague. I want to feel more specific, to live a specified life, yet I think vague can be good. To never lose myself is to never force myself to do the finding. I must play with time and space. Words are a play with time and space. Words are the measuring beam against which all things are placed. Let my world, you, fall into place. I wonder how much space I take up, if a thought can take up secondary space.

With love,
M

My dear world,

I wonder if you would agree with me that *slip* is a very good word. *Slip* is currently my favorite word, though I have never had a favorite word before. Maybe *slip* is my new favorite word because all the lovely intangibles can slip into your life without your noticing until the slip of your being realizes it is so. Maybe it is because I have a need to slip my life into you in ways unknown, maybe because you, world, are a slip of a word. Maybe because it relates to the way one wants to live, leaving an imprint but no more, maybe because I like the way bodies can slip into one another, maybe because a slip as a garment is ever contradictory, a container yet not. A slippage, what has not come to pass or what has passed, a bit of noth-ingness or a bit of everything if one considers all a slip of paper might hold. The word *slip* contains and offers itself. Maybe one should aspire to be a slip, to slip.

With love,
M

My dear world,

You seem centered, but maybe it all comes down to the aside. Gravitating slightly to the left and slightly to the right. Maybe life with you is a doing away with things. Looking without we see within, a simultaneous expansion and contraction. Like letters taking shape on the page, life makes its way. We gather ourselves up into loose clouds, or rather faraway stars that when viewed are just a little bit off. Maybe one can gather up all the parts of oneself that want to be free. We make such a fuss about being free of others, but maybe we simply need to be free of ourselves — or at least live as if it is possible.

With love,
M

My dear world,

I know a young woman who tired of herself because she was so much herself, excessively so. She practiced making a shadow of the quiet bits of herself, slipping away for a time into the abyss of the unknown, a dark, reflectionless place, but was never quite satisfied with the overall effect. Once, as this slippage of a being, she felt an overwhelming urge to abandon the solidity of herself in a mad dash for freedom, salvation that rested in the arms of a nonidentity, yet she feared the drifting life, an existence in which air tumbles through a body and makes one feel too absent for comfort, in a dimension slightly away from whatever central plane might hold everything together. And so she always returned to herself and was glad, if also wondrous, a mass of pondering bits considering aboutness, the things that tremble outside the periphery in regions we do not dare to explore.

With love,
M

My dear world,

I present to you a series of leanings. These letters of mine
to you are meaning enclosed in sound, in the feel of the
tongue, the open and close of the mouth. Each of my
sentences is a little experiment that can go wrong by not
exploding in the proper way. I am wondering why you
do not respond to my many missives, but a thought
dropped into my head the other day: that you will somehow birth a sentence for every one of the hairs on my
head, each sentence faithful to the length and texture of
its obstinate strand. I am not quite sure how to interpret
this, but I have a certain intuition that you, my world,
are not entirely unaware. I do get anxious sometimes. I
ask for your forgiveness if I have presumed your lack of
obvious participation a potential problem. Please know
I hope that you will respond to me, but I understand if
you are too busy.

With love,
M

My dear world,

I wonder if I could write a book on us. If I were to write a book, a memoir of all the humdrum and intrigue, this is how I would begin: "This book has not yearned to be written. It is not one of those books that bursts out of one's lungs in exhalation, but rather one that offers itself as a kind of tangential thought or remark as one sits in the park." Like everyone else, I guess when it comes down to it, all I am trying to do here is to construct myself, going along. I am engaged in the act of construction. I like to think I am more than what may have happened to me, that I can happen to you, too. I must go out to live for a time. But I will linger here for a while more, for it is nice to have a reflecting ground, and you, dear world, have some solidity about you.

With love,
M

~ II ~

Easing forth

My dear world,

Maybe I am indebted to the mystery I come from. Maybe I became acquainted with you, world, a little sooner than some. I should think easing forth is easier when one comes from a mystery, for one has nothing and everything to look back upon. This prepares one for the future, which also holds the possibility of nothing and everything. And it seems that the here and now is simply that, nothing more or less. I came, at a young age, to an understanding that what may seem like abandonment can be an act of love. Of other things, too, but maybe when having a child is a crime, when one must leave what came of her behind, it is the ultimate test of love. I have realized that leaving things and people behind can work out in ways one would not realize, when one acts aligned with what one feels is right even when it seems all too wrong. Dear world, please know she left me in sunshine.

With love,
M

My dear world,

There is a little valley that is like a small golden cloud,
full of wheat fields and winding roads and shady oaks.
The wind in this valley makes a wholesome sound that
makes you feel close to the earth. I do not come from
this place, though I am familiar with a place like it. I come
from mounds of red, orange, and green, and a bit of rain,
from middles and halves, like long socks that only go so
far. I am between the cloud and the leaf, hovering over
you, world. My worded wings offer you the possibility
of my displaced self. I am almost asking, waiting, for my
wings to drop away. I would be free, then. I would re-
side less inside the mind. You would find me a solid body
ready to meet yours. You would find me significant in my
insignificance. No, though, I am not the lost daughter of
Daedalus, only perhaps a lost daughter, and my words
do nothing but drift in open spaces of paper hoping to
be bodies, valleys, leaves.

With love,
M

My dear world,

If I could be from anywhere, maybe I would like to be from the sky or the sea, for I am familiar with the periphery, at home in it. The periphery is love. Like the moon aglow from afar. I consider myself and feel I can relate to the world's slants, embrace the perfection of what some may deem imperfect. I think of love and realize it cannot be thought of. Like light, cannot be held in one's arms. Maybe certain things like love and light and beauty can only be felt? I tell myself that beauty is so often accepted for what it is except when it is the kind that takes one by surprise, and then we find that beauty has been marginalized. I wonder if a baby raised on love can turn out all right. I would say so. I should hope you agree with me, my love.

With love,
M

My dear world,

I always thought if I had a previous life it must have been rather poor because this life is so good to me. I think — I must have done all right before, in that other life. Then the fear takes hold — maybe I will not live up to things as well this time. I am not always loving, not always kind, and my words are a silvery hope. But I think, ultimately, one must not think like this — it is too much thinking. That is probably too often the problem. One must simply go on, in the movement of moments. It is natural to go along in moments, to think in moments, to measure in moments, to see that everything has a thousand moments, that we have an unlimited surplus of moments. To believe in moments makes life endless, no?

With love,
M

My dear world,

I remember rocking in the light-blue wicker chair. Sitting in my mother's lap, curling beneath her shirt, peeking my head out, birthing myself into life. I brought myself into the world over and over again. At the time, I did not understand I came from another belly and she had traveled overseas to bring me to her own. All I knew was that this was how I had come into the world. I wonder if, when you do not have words, you feel more. That was a time of wordless wonder, a time when everything was a mystery except that I did not know it in words. I knew what it was to peer into the light, look up, and see her smiling eyes. It was something good.

With love,
M

My dear world,

What you offer is not exactly luck. I remember waking
sobbing at dreams of my new mother dead. I remember
waiting by a certain window so often, fearing news of her
death. I remember writing to my old mother in a journal
bought by my new mother, only to cast it aside. What
is and is not pour forth and we accept and love and fear.
We feel in nuanced ways. We collect gestures to respond.
Mine was a childhood of normalcy, and, yes, of fathom-
ing the dictionary definition of adoption — until it was
not. It would seem we all live in a state of adoption. One
may adopt a place, a person, a way of being, and, also,
one may be adopted by a place, a person, a way of being.
We adopt and are adopted. We are creatures of adoption.
But I would name it life more than luck.

With love,
M

My dear world,

In the bad dream, it is more the edge of an atmosphere I recall. There is a wheel of some sort — something going round and round that will not stop for me, or maybe I am not able to stop for it. I continued to emerge from something horrible, but I do not know what it is. The primary feeling is helplessness, an inability to move forth from a particular state of being. Later, I will write that we live in movement. I think that dream encompasses my terror of existing in a static state, of repetition when it has stopped being beautiful, of Sisyphus and his rock. The opposite of aesthetically pleasing. (Can one lead an aesthetically pleasing life?) My most joyous dreams involve flight, in which my body is movement itself — I move in a second atmosphere. To live in movement on the feet, on wings, in the mind, is the best thing. To rest a few thoughts on the toes in a walk, on a drifting in the air, in the space of unfamiliar atmosphere.

With love,
M

My dear world,

I think I am fairly ripened and I am glad. "Thank them for letting you ripen," my landlady once told me. "You were meant to be here," she said. My landlady told me that she came into the world with her feet dangling in the waters of a toilet. Her mother thought she had a stomachache, but instead she was giving birth. My landlady was raised by a stranger after her mother left and her grandmother died. "Look at us here, in this city, talking, in this kitchen!" she said to me. "We were meant to be here and that makes us special," she said. Dear world, I am glad to be here with you, though I know I am not special — it is an intuition over a series of moments. But I do know you hold us all in your earth arms, offering a landing like the toilet my landlady was birthed into.

With love,
M

My dear world,

I am beginning to think that perhaps bodies are merely matter formed of secret. A part of me will always grasp for what is not there, a landscape in that fiercely feeling part of the body. I will always believe the way we move through time is the way wings move through air, with infinite possibility ever in a moment. I will adopt her obsessions, and his, and yours. I will walk cemeteries, little bits of sun and shadow floating about in my head. I will lack style, seeking too much to vaguen or specify myself, when in fact the ideal probably exists in the balance between the two. I will seek something true inside the most vulnerable parts of myself. I will always realize that you are a stranger to me.

With love,
M

My dear world,

There have been times I found it physically hard to speak. Something stole snippets of my breath. The words would catch, I would find it painful to identify the time to take a breath, I would wonder and feel inadequate. I would choose to be silent so as not to be embarrassed. I held on to silence like it would save me. Sometimes, still, I find it difficult to speak and breathe. A person can get lost trying to find a home in herself — but then you simply begin to go on as one must go on, and maybe you say a little something to yourself every once in a while just to practice being with words, meeting silence, meeting yourself again, and maybe you frequent empty rooms to familiarize yourself with the meaning of space as in a blank page, and yourself in it, and maybe you scribble like this will help you come home to yourself, but eventually you fit things together, and what made no sense finds its way into something plausible by virtue of its sheer existence. As one goes on, one learns how to hone an intuition for you, of course.

With love,
M

My dear world,

There always is something to be said, but the challenge is finding the person of the many persons in you to say that something and to figure out just how fragmented you are, and then to experiment with visions of wholeness that will enable further experiments of comprehensible speech. You make the necessary adjustments and try to fit forms together, and it is hard because you do not know the forms until they have worked themselves out into what one might want to call shapes on the edge of the unsaid, but then ta-da: there comes into being something you recognize as yourself and the strange words that come out. When this happens you are astonished and a little frightened because it is like everything that was possible was put aside in that moment in favor of something else, and you are reminded of things lost: words left wanting a paper home, lost love, a host of other definitively melancholy things ready to be longed for. You begin to blather.

With love,
M

My dear world,

The number of aches a body has been through — and yet
we still hold together as flesh, blood, bone. Some folks
have more aches, concentrated masses that accumulate
over the years: sculpted, invisible, deeply felt. I do not
think I have more or less than average. And then, too, the
number of dreams a body has been through — for the
body is a house of dreams, as well. These dreams are concentrated in a particularly airy way (the more dreams, the
lighter the body becomes), and one must remember that
when one holds another, one holds that other's dreams
in her arms. We are all made of soft, drooping parts, yet
so much sky there is too. I am glad to report that I have
found that a gentle person — a body fully acquainted
with aches and dreams — always comes along.

With love,
M

My dear world,

I wonder if there has been a book written on toes — the bottom parts of a body are just as important as the top parts. Each chapter would focus on one of the ten toes and each would inspire singular, existential commentary: the potential of our toes as leaders, the solidity of our little instruments, the dangers of relating size and value. It would be called *The Toe Manifesto* and people would be interested in reading it because, after all, it is the toe that goes forward first and foremost, and the toe that helps to tell us if our bodies are hot or cold — in other words, the toe experiences far more than we give it credit for.

With love,
M

My dear world,

I write to you having been stung by a bee. The unfortunate toe swells with indignation, and it feels like my heart is doing a little tap dance in my foot. The venom is spreading to make my toes plump, red, itchy masses of flesh. I am reminded of what I am. I have read that bee venom can help arthritis and has other medicinal properties in addition to the excruciating pain it can cause. I will try to remember this in later years, applying venom to my various hurting parts. In the meantime, I sit here thankful for frozen watermelon and antihistamines. I contemplate the importance of occasional pain and feel grateful I have nothing to do but be for several days. I need some practice at that.

With love,
M

My dear world,

We seem to make our heads look attractive with hats to conceal, to enhance, to make them look more or less imposing than they really are. I recommend the French beret, for it gives the impression of just the right soft toughness, a veritable wave of sophisticated brain matter. It is the kind of hat that inspires a person to grow into it, to become the person they never knew they could be. The space between the top of the head and the beginnings of hat is among the most intimate of areas: earlobe behinds, elbow insides, and anuses. One must pay heed to such spaces for they hold a potential not fully known (but generally agreed to be vast). I think you, world, must know this, with your skies and seas, and that you may approve of our sometimes seemingly silly-but-not-quite aspirings.

With love,
M

My dear world,

Sometimes I like to practice going about on sleep. Going about on sleep, I do not recall the shapes my pen ought to make, the ways my heart and brain ought to take. Nothing is coherent. Thoughts come and go and I am left with myself, my intuition for forward movement and wide, sloppy words, working feeling into freedom. And then a restedness, pure selfhood, like the world, you — you are my own once again. I forge an immortality of odd bits and ends fit for every sized life. I fit myself together and hope you can read me, at least a little, or make the attempt in good spirit. It will be as if we are looking at one another in a dusty mirror, side by side, as if we are living within and without the bounds of punctuation. We will live and love together by always being slightly at odds.

With love,
M

My dear world,

There is nothing quite like yearning for sleep. You feel the waiting in your body, a still and moving mass. I tire of waiting, writing, to you sometimes, and it is like this yearning for sleep. As much as I may be in love with you, I know I can go love others. Now I do not think it is wise to fall in love more than a thousand times, but it is certainly possible. I want to protect my heart a little, though. I will practice patience. I will go and take some naps. Ah, but the ways my body turns, thinking of you, in reflexes of want. I cannot help but generate love like it will save me from loss. Thinking of you I am reminded that sometimes something can be excessively true. I hope you will write me a poem one day because that is the truest thing you could do.

With love,
M

My dear world,

Consider when a dream rests at the tippy toes of your memory and you have only a vague sense of it, your body tense and vibrating with the desire to know that which remains just out of reach. I think if I remember correctly, this is what it is like to be a child wanting to know what it is like to be what you perceive as an adult. And upon pondering this, I think perhaps the best time to be a child is as an adult. I would like to do more in appreciating the mindset of the child. Maybe it has something to do with taking ourselves very seriously and with great disregard, as well as having a healthy dose of awe and doubt for all else.

With love,
M

My dear world,

It was not a dream and I was not a child. I will always have those regrets, those little terrible beings of regret. You will never like all the people you once were, I tell myself. But I hope I am getting to be more attuned to feeling, to those alive beside me. Perhaps it is not impossible to practice love. I sense a beginning, the depreciation of spelling, scooping into intuitive clusters of words rather than their lettered components. The more I read, the less I speak — any meaning accrued through speaking is accidental, it would seem. I do not want to live to the rhythm of an offbeat heart, though I know it is a fault.

With love,
M

My dear world,

I found a box of little Chinese clothes in my old closet. "Yao was estimated to be 6 days old when she was left / found / placed in a small town or country part of the province of Anhui, in central China." The clothes used to fit a girl with a different name, a girl with flaming cheeks. "She had such a wonderful laugh. And teeth!" It was not the Scandinavian couple that would adopt Yao, but an American woman. The woman who sat with her on the floor of a Chinese hotel to peruse an assortment of toys. "I decided right then that we would be all right together." And they are all right. Later, Yao comes to know a singular sweetness. She comes to feel the presence of home — not a home in the likeness of the mother's womb, but as a place of rest for the body, the blood, the head, the heart — like a little closet for little clothes.

With love,
M

～ III ～

In light of all those other lives

My dear world,

I am sitting here thinking about where I am, relatively
speaking. That is, my general self-hood and situation in
life in light of all those other lives. And yet I continue
to think of how I miss you — love and longing are so
odd — to think just a small thought of you makes my
fatigue seem to move a good distance away. I am ready
to go to sleep — I keep feeling ready to go to sleep. Is it
that I feel alone? Maybe this is the appropriate time to
consider the possibility and to make peace with it. There
is nothing stopping me from trying to enjoy eating that
piece of fruit there, is there? It must be only myself.

With love,
M

My dear world,

The birds have different beaks here, bright orange like they contain the sun and long like the needle thorns found on trees. Yes, you could pick a thorn from a tree and use it as a needle here. Here, you can hold a tree and cradle it in your arms, like a lonely child. This is a place dancing with children, like scattered sunlight. Avocados taste like vegetable butter. Concepts have become lives. The lives here! The bodies, the smiles, the eyes. Living here, the ears know before the eyes — of fire and rain, for instance — and, too, a body feels safer out of light, held by darkness. I am a bundle of yearning for home, yet I already know a yearning for all I will leave behind.

With love,
M

My dear world,

They ask me for love stories almost every day. I think we
are all looking for love stories in our hearts, but folks here
seem to be more forward in their wants. I think I would
like to write a book on love because one cannot speak of
it too much. *A Small Study on Love. A Survey of Love.
An Investigation of Love. A Compendium on Love. An
Omnibus on Love. The Forms of Love. An Opus on Love.
Portraits of Love. To Love and to Be Loved.* I see a young
woman striding down the street and I wonder if she is
in a hurry to love. I wonder if there will ever come a day
when people can exchange hearts.

With love,
M

My dear world,

The waitress does not ask, "Can I get you anything else?"
or "Are you all set?" Instead, she asks, "Are you happy?"
Given all they say about happiness and its various
manifestations, I think I can claim I am indeed happy.
In a few moments I cannot be sure, but in this particular
moment, there is a little space bumping about in my heart
that seems to make it feel more open, fuller than usual.
And this makes my eyes and nose and smile open up
wider as well. Even the tips of my fingers moving with the
air are more welcoming. When there is nothing else, I can
always lay myself down, for a bit. I can let my hopes
wander the horizon and my dreams navigate the clouds.
I can rest my mind on the sure lines of the hills here and
even stretch out upon that mountain. I can think silly
thoughts like this.

With love,
M

My dear world,

A quiet, sunlit room is a lovely thing to return to. I realize this more as I grow older. Sun is the best company for solitude. One need not speak in such a room, only let the eyes breathe beauty. It is when one is in a sun-filled room one begins to understand the notion of paradise, where the most present being is light. Nothing needs to be said or heard or understood. Life lies beneath everything, in all the bits of light that have hidden themselves in the room. A sunlit room has the tendency to make me feel alive in a way altogether more tender than one might realize.

With love,
M

My dear world,

When I have not been outside for a while, I must get accustomed to existing outside my head. The patterns of people on streets, the cold shadows of buildings, the sounds of humans. I must get used to reading shoes and haircuts and abandon thoughts like that everything looks more beautiful when it is beneath a puddle of clear water. I try to engage like any person who has not shut herself in a sunlit room for hours at a time, and I think I do well at it, though sometimes I may be distant. Dreams may be of the day and of the night, unusual in their prolific presence and startling absence.

With love,
M

My dear world,

I was in the library, hugged by books, but I did not know what a hug was until the child. When she came and put her arms around me, I knew to put my arms around her as well — to make a hug. I felt pleased with myself. And then she — a girl who was not five feet — lifted me. She spun around. My toes traveled about, a glorious few inches from the ground. I squealed and knew helplessness and delight for several seconds. When I stood upright, I expressed my appreciation, donned my decade or two with a smile. I wonder, when we spin, if it is practice for identifying the essential. You must know a thing or two about that, my dear.

With love,
M

My dear world,

They call this place of yours "complex" like it is a disease. Maybe it will be the simple things that help to make it into a better kind of complexity, like the little girls with their hugs. They looked at me, shy and eager, and when I looked at them, away, and back again, I knew they saw the same shy eagerness in my face. They came up to me then, and — with an encouraging smile — hugged me, one by one. I embraced their little bodies like I knew how, and I think they believed. A hug from a group of stranger girls is not something everyone knows, though it is probably the kind of thing that heals the world.

With love,
M

My dear world,

I was never very good at being myself. Too much exposure to too many people does not make this easier. One could argue that such exposure allows one to make a more complete discovery of the self by process of elimination, but I am finding that it simply makes me want to go to sleep, to go away somehow, to put the self on hold. I think, being here, the chief danger is forgetting who I am. I thought I was ready to be destabilized, to leave myself at the door, but it turns out that I am rather attached to the concept of myself. Which reminds me — I don't believe I have yet seen a person who looks Chinese. I will look at myself in the mirror more often to compensate.

With love,
M

My dear world,

The hairs keep falling out — they collect on the carpet and form airy clumps over time. One must use the fingers and a piece of tape to scrape up the strands for discarding. It is gruesome to see them all in a pile, the remnants of yourself that you unwittingly leave behind. They sit, floating, a massive heap in the toilet bowl. They are like bad memories that nobody else ever formed or that everyone has forgotten, memories that only you will keep. I keep seeing them, one more, and another. How does one go on? I must learn to live with those discarded imperfections, those strands that will not quite go. I must lovingly pick them up and know that not all remnants are so. I must remember to discard them in the garbage bin instead, or better yet, give them to the birds.

With love,
M

My dear world,

I miss winter. Winter makes everything feel more real. I left some lovely folks behind. The oddest are the loveliest. Blankets of prose and pocketfuls of snow, I lengthened my eyes for the long view and closed them to see the obvious. I lived alongside words unsaid. Now I am here, waiting for you and myself, and I can leave us both behind, but I am equally ready to propel myself into whatever joy we have at our disposal. I have resigned myself to a state between waiting and waking, in which one can wait for a long length of time and then realize one has stopped waiting only to wake up to life. In this summer heat, I must remember that the realest things are the closest and farthest away, like the warmth found in winter: the heat hidden in the folds of one's coat, a lost floating breath, a kiss across the distance of zero degrees.

With love,
M

My dear world,

Sometimes being here, living, is exhausting. Maybe it is the new place and the new faces, but maybe, also, it is the way people look at me so I am always somehow on guard, alive in a lesser way. Maybe they wonder how to interpret me because the facts are not so ingrained in their history. One woman tells me she once dated a Taiwanese man after her husband died, though she does not say much more about him except that he was kind. I have a sneaking suspicion that I am the second Asian-looking person she has known — though I do find it sweet when people try to relate. I suppose I could try to make a good impression, but I think perhaps I will simply be as much of myself as I want and live as best I can. It helps that I have realized I am not very good at being someone other than myself. I have tried and obviously failed, and I am glad because it was a very tiresome experience.

With love,
M

My dear world,

I should mention that I received a marriage proposal. At the time, though, I did not hear it — all I heard from the man was that he would be nice to me and not make me cry. Later someone informed me — and I was surprised to hear — there had been talk of marriage. Please rest assured that every morning I think of you, and the only thing keeping me company in my hours alone is the smell of ripe peaches. I know you expect I will meet another, but please know I remain passionately committed to you. In fact, I hope you do not think I miss you excessively, and I hope I love you in amounts appropriate to all you have expressed for me, as I do not want to create an imbalance in this relationship.

With love,
M

My dear world,

Sometimes I must remind myself that I am rather novel to everyone I meet here — a foreign concept. This can be powerful. It can be tiring, but the sky can be a very generous place to rest the eyes sometimes. I inhabit myself in a rather distant way. I wish that I could hold you. I scratch my scalp in circular motions, and what results occasionally drifts off and away like snow. Little suns form behind my eyes and a general weariness rests about the mouth and corners of the eyes. The sun, like snow, can be both gentle and harsh. One is moved to wishes and whys. There are so many things to wish, though I mostly keep my wishes inside. Being here, I know some fortune in being foreign.

With love,
M

My dear world,

After the fire, we peek out the window into the night for long seconds, hoping to see a fire-setting chicken thief. I watch the yellow light go on and off and try to sense anything that feels like a field set on fire. Come morning, we walk a windy canvas of ash, putting out smoking plastic and smoldering grass. A never-ending quest to quench the possibility of orange. The sky is milky white, so promising. I begin to realize why a person might like to pray. I wonder if I should fill my bathtub just in case. I sleep with glasses on. I think, when we hear the wind rushing through the trees, we feel our souls or spirits or something, some *thing* in us reflected way up there in the sky where the air and green are mixing, dance of branch and leaf.

With love,
M

My dear world,

I wonder if you know what is true. Maybe, like a tracker, all one can do is study the spoors between self and sun. Maybe the limits of truth lie in the imagination one projects onto signs. Truth exists in the relationship between self, signs, sun. The self, the world of signs, that elusive ideal. Those instants when possibilities become plausible and suspicions become realizations, when we confuse the signs and the sun and our feet. Truth is found in forgetting ourselves and becoming something else, returning to life again and again in its different forms. Or maybe it's simply feeling the sun's burn.

With love,
M

My dear world,

They told me five preachers would come to visit, though
none were preachers — simply four girls and a boy with a
loaf of bread, milk, lasagna, and wine. The kitchen even
provided a tray of thirty eggs. In the living room, my
guests asked me to clarify "agnosticism" versus
"atheism," and I asked them if it was "charismatic" like
the adjective. Later, we went into town for waffles and
ice cream. High school boys in uniforms of navy blue
and white stripes looked on, smiling. I had thought they
were circus performers when I first arrived. In the morning I woke to the sight of eight eggs less and twenty-two
more. I hope to see my visitors again on their return.

With love,
M

My dear world,

She asked me what I had learned since my arrival. "Hmm," I replied. "I guess I have learned that people can be both racist and kind," I said. I did not say that there is a trembling rage that has not yet transformed from shock when these kind people say, "Black people don't work hard." I did say that people who can hold pencils in their hair are not less than those who cannot. I said I had thought of people in simple terms, but realized it was somewhat of a lost cause after I told someone he was a racist while he was drunk. I think I am slower to talk, even slower than the slow I was before, for I will never know where someone comes from, of love and of loss, and I can write now, thinking back, that wondering has no cost.

With love,
M

My dear world,

Since I had left the church, had I found some other way
to practice, she asked. "Hmm," I replied. "I have turned
to words," I said. "And try to live a good life," I added.
I felt a little inadequate. But really, I was thinking of my
paper cranes, folding them over and over, every slip of
paper a piece of potential, trying to create a more
beautiful world. And isn't that what religion is for, I
should have thought and said, like one prayer or one
blessing at a time, an invisible force of feeling and good.

With love,
M

My dear world,

At the farm, like here on this spot of lit land, I felt a certain version of freedom. I woke to the donkey's bray and the rooster's crow and the sun peeping into windows. The wind joined me like a friend and showed me how living on trees and grass could be like living on wings. I climbed the barn roof and lay on the warm shingles, letting my body soak in the sun. Being in the country is like being in a dream — one doesn't quite know who one is. There is an anonymity to it all — that strange human creature that is me, one among all. There on the farm as a child, I had a pile of short and long sticks by the door to throw for the dog. I never wanted to run away by hiding in a box. This place is like that in some ways, fire and all.

With love,
M

⁓ IV ⁓

Embracing language like unrequited love

My dear world,

Are there not moments you wish language did not exist? That you could simply sing a sound or hum a hum or embrace in earnest affection? Language cannot express, for instance — of course — a love. I could say I loved him so much sometimes I forgot his name. That when I looked at him I felt my eyes glowing. But you, world, will always be language-less. For language means nothing, often — too often — and I suppose I will live with this and accept the inadequacy of my many missives. I will treat language with resigned delight, embrace it like unrequited love, offer words to you with a kind of secret shame, for I know that sometimes there is such a thing as too much language, and that language can hold a kind of sincerity that is tiresome and overwrought.

With love,
M

My dear world,

I am concerned I do not always realize I am alive and, moreover, that I live more in language than in life. That thought obliquely terrifies me. But I think when I write I let myself become soft and open, and that I feel more loving when I write. Forgive me for saying so, but I want to live beautifully, like a painting, in subtle brushstrokes, like you, because maybe beauty can aspire to truth even if it is not. Or maybe one has simply to aspire to create something beautiful, practice a particular slant of thought and being. Or maybe, after all, something ugly is in order, and one realizes the blending of all things like the sky and the land or the land and the sea. Maybe one must surrender to one's life, the serendipity of things, as with the sky and the land and the sea.

With love,
M

My dear world,

I think maybe if you are raised in relative solitude, you tend to seek it more in life. Solitude becomes the medium for exploring thought in the most thorough way. Exploring what can emerge from varying layers of solitude: solitude on solitude. You become almost too acquainted with the abstract. Solitude lets one look at things long enough so that they drift out of focus then look at them again. I let quiet shape what I say, then realize there is nothing that can be fully said — the reason for gestures and eyes and art. Always something waiting, wanting, expectant, yet also curiously not.

With love,
M

My dear world,

It would seem that the kinds of experiences I seek, even
though I may not always seem to know it, tend to be the
ones that will bruise me so that I put a hand out to you
in awe, the ones that make me feel as though I have been
experienced out of myself, the ones that are so large and
so small and so significant in their insignificant signifi-
cance, I feel I should revere them more than I do. Then
I realize experience cannot be measured — there are no
measures. I try to gauge the fatigue of the various moments involved, to determine the worth of said experiences, and then think: I once knew a young girl who did
not know what to do with you, world, though you were
fairly offered to her at her feet.

With love,
M

My dear world,

This morning I took a bath and I can still smell the scent of soap on my skin. I remember how I sunk into the tub, letting it hold me, the water inching up to my neck with a patient touch. Lying there, quiet like the little animal I am or want to be, I stared across the distance of my body to my toes, pressing against the edge of the end of the tub peeking out of the water. And I think, now, that perhaps it is not all too bad a metaphor for how we ought to move through life. Our bodies gentle and ready for love, our heads and toes ready to explore the varying landscapes of the world.

With love,
M

My dear world,

If I do not find something better to do soon, I shall grow
pale and plump at my desk in a graveyard of old words.
I shall grow wholeheartedly lethargic living in my lovely
land of haze. I like the thought a lot. Maybe if I grow
nice and large, I will be kindlier and more comfortable,
growing accustomed to the dynamics of ambling about.
I think I would make a very nice large person as long as
my movement was not too restricted by the enormity of
my thighs. For I would have ample thighs, larger than
the large they are now, and they would propel my sizable
being into hearts and minds by virtue of their serenely
confident curves. But alas, I will not be growing larger
anytime soon, for I must arise to go to school.

With love,
M

My dear world,

When I spend a certain amount of time with a person, I begin to see them less and less in a physical respect. I become more attuned to how their presence emanates into mine and mine into theirs, so the moments are full of our togetherness. I become more attuned to our shared words — the words we exchange, have exchanged, will exchange. I have begun to believe there is no great love without words — the words that rest between two lovers like a secret create a third world between the worlds of their bodies. Words serve as memory, and I take joy in these so-called derivatives, in the veiled loveliness of my twenty-six letters all lined up in a row. Hoping for some from you, soon.

With love,
M

My dear world,

I have begun to think, and, if it is not too presumptuous to say, to realize, that those who write and read live much longer lives. The danger in this is that one must be wary of extending one's life in words too long, for there must always be a balance between a life in pages and that other elusive life none have yet learned. Everything in moderation, as the saying goes. I think as I go along, I must wean myself off words and begin to make motions toward the teats of the world. Yet I wonder — perhaps words can very well be the teats of the world, you, the conduit through which I live and learn. I have found that I cannot be away from them for too long.

With love,
M

My dear world,

I love you for your lack of specificity. It is hard for me to embrace the specific. For me, the broad is beautiful. The smudge of what is there and what is absent embraces the in-between of specificity and universality, and so we have the bliss of imperfection, of curves, of movement around what it is we really yearn to say, so yearning itself is encompassed in all its raw bits. Maybe an earnest portrayal of yearning is ever something beautiful, feels true. I try to live in the luminosity of things. I believe the arrangement of the sounds in words is what allows me to write a sentence without feeling overly ashamed of its inadequacy. For even if the sentence is horribly wrong, at the very least it is not too much of an offense to the human ears — I have tested it upon my own, and survived! It is these notions, of vagueness, of sound, that speak most meaningfully to me. I wonder if that is what a life is. A vague smudge, a yearning, a series of notes that may or may not come together in harmony.

With love,
M

My dear world,

The ears seem to be among the most sensitive parts of the body. Imagine what the right sounds, the right words, arranged in sentences and bits, can do to them. As one who does not quite know what to say, lyricism is my way of slipping into the wanting to say something. Lyricism is the language of desire, of falling in love with life. If realism is capturing, lyricism is seduction, the paying of a compliment to life. In lyricism words are not a means to an end. Rather, they are the end itself, beating with the beauty of life. I want to be conscious of the beat of every word, for the way of a word relates to the world the kind of form one wants to make. And so lyricism seems to be an act of capturing the self. I am starting to get the feeling I was born into love and lyricism, and I sense something lyrical about you, too.

With love,
M

My dear world,

I grow skeptical of myself. Maybe it is easier to be skeptical when one is sad. I have an aesthetic attraction toward you, world, but sometimes I wonder. As with reading, sometimes, when I find myself contemplating the potential of a text to corrupt, leading me to discover entirely new angles of thought, ones I never wanted to know before. There is an uneasy wondrousness. And, of course, I wonder if I wonder too much or not enough, and I wonder at my wonderings and if they are sufficient. One wishes one's stuttered breaths could write the words out, one hopes the heavy pull of one's eyes makes one wise, one feels that the bend of one's body and head could fit earth so well.

With love,
M

My dear world,

Sometimes I wish I could sweep myself away from myself for a small break. Perhaps I must simply position my eyes correctly, and then I will see in the way I want but do not realize because I forgot. I must focus them in just the way they were meant to be focused, and I must remember to recall what is forward and what is behind. And I must not forget to be silent at the right times. Sometimes I think that maybe my awful eyes were meant simply for existing in my head and my hands, for wandering the house within the head, stopping in all those little rooms for rest, for leaning into the concavity of the page, never really wanting to go back.

With love,
M

My dear world,

I like to hang my laundry at night, standing among the stars. The wet clothes, the silky sky, the pinpoints of light let me know I am alive. That I should continue breathing or stop at any moment seems inevitable. I feel ready to be. Hanging my laundry, I prepare it to go out into the world again to become dirty, to realize sometimes living can be hard. I prepare a part of myself. Maybe a piece of washed clothing is like a sheet of paper, a slip of the body, a remnant of the self. It is soothing to place it on the line just so, drifting in space and wind, a part of you hovering above earth. If I could simply place the various parts of myself into the night sky to occasionally glance up and behold myself — maybe in the end I am only hoping to vicariously soak up some starlight.

With love,
M

My dear world,

Is feeling always true? Is that why we gravitate toward poets, those of a feeling nature? Are they the truest beings? Feeling beings, joining the disparate. Poets usually are the kind of folk who like to go on walks because they feel like it, not because they must go somewhere. In other words, purpose is less a contaminating factor when considering a poet. What if we had a poet for a president? I should think a poet could address our world's woes. A poet's home generally consists of mounds of books, the smells of them all falling gently into one another, like country air. I should think a poet president would be able to create the same kind of home, a delectable confluence of various spaces. A poet is most political.

With love,
M

My dear world,

I am trying to learn to look askance. I prefer daydreaming with my gaze resting on air — where the sky fills the spaces between buildings, in the flutter of wings, nested within passion accentuated by distance, et cetera — for it is easier than daydreaming with the gaze resting on earth. To look into space sharpens one's ability to pierce the invisible life between words and sentences and to be comfortable with moments one does not know what to do with. I practice being blind. And I need practice because one of my greatest fears is to be blind, you know; but then one might also say I fear life. To not see is *not* to not fully be — to know your placement is impermanent, a smudge off and away — for this is in fact life precisely.

With love,
M

My dear world,

Maybe every artwork seeks to place one in a liminal space, to displace. Liminality is a coming and a going, an in-between-ness. Displacement allows for a barely there realization of something new about one's existence. Maybe art is essential because it is the smallest way of letting a person experience a kind of nonexistence or re-existence. That is, it is the least extreme version of experiencing one's impending death. I think every person ought to wonder at least once, "Will I die now?" Then, ideally, they will go on living. Art allows us to die over and over without actually dying. Only we must catch our breath.

With love,
M

My dear world,

Sometimes, waking, I will not remember who I am. That is to say, I have no sense of my place in you, world, why I lie in this particular spot and wake at this particular time and if the feelings I feel are indeed the feelings that belong to the person I supposedly am. It will take me some immeasurable number of moments to recognize my existence for what it is and piece the details of my waking life together. Each time I will feel startled, meeting myself in my mind and body like this. I will experience a brief relief tinged by sadness that I am no longer quite a mystery.

With love,
M

My dear world,

Every once in a while, and it happens only several times a year if I am lucky, I will feel astonishment that I exist, that I am sitting, standing, perceiving, and that others perceive me. It will occur to me that my particular situation in life and in being alive is a very strange fact, and then it will occur to me that it is so easy to slip away into nonexistence, into neutrality. And then I will go on with my day and forget I exist with all my senses and opportunities to infringe on others' existence until the next time it occurs to me I exist. It is probably a good thing I am not always so aware of my existence because otherwise I would walk about in a haze of wonder embracing things. I think it is good to become accustomed to existing without thinking about it on a constant basis, but I do feel very fortunate to occasionally realize my presence here.

With love,
M

My dear world,

I have been thinking about what reading can mean, and
what it means for us. Maybe reading is what one does
to inflict a thousand feelings upon the self, a shortcut to
looking into another's eyes and feeling their life, a way
to ready oneself for becoming a different kind of person, a means of teaching oneself how to live, to practice breathing without reason or rather need for reason,
a lens through which to consider the logistics of people,
a means of nurturing an attraction to the theory of life, a
way of learning how to alter the landscape of one's heart,
et cetera. Maybe one reads because the text is seductive,
just as one's gaze gravitates toward a photograph, figure,
or film that sufficiently seduces. When one reads, one en-
gages in the textual alternative or precursor to sex. That
is why a person can never be read immediately and we
must try to take our time in reading one another.

With love,
M

My dear world,

I had a dream about asking someone how he was and his response of "not okay." I wish more people would respond like this. We could so easily bare our souls to one another. We want to, I know we want to, just like we want to use the word "soul" except that we were once forbidden to. I know this because I have been on a subway platform. A subway platform offers just enough space to properly, indecorously stare. There always is a moment in which a person may stare across the space of an absent or windowed train to catch another's gaze. If only we always had these spaces for nakedness available to us. I suppose that is what dreams are for, though. I dream of you often, my dear — and you are splendidly naked.

With love,
M

ᴠ

To love a stranger

My dear world,

Every morning I birth an image of you in my stomach. Sometimes I do not know who you are, you are so removed. I wish I could wrap my arms about you and squeeze you into myself, and then I would know you. Although everyone knows it is the easiest thing to love a stranger. I have such feeling, but nowhere to place it. I find it difficult to go to sleep, to dream properly. I am always readying myself, though I know not what for. I sit in the corners of rooms where I can best be in the recesses, let the room press into my body, gradually understand that I must be ever unidentifiable to myself or else I would have to seriously question my presence. For there is no going on if I cannot constantly reimagine myself as making motions away from the center and toward you. We must be sufficiently mysterious.

With love,
M

My dear world,

It has occurred to me that men and women are more beautiful in the cold. Perhaps one can feel their warmth more in lower temperatures, unjust a statement as that may be. Maybe they stand a little taller, a little stiffer, and when you take the arm of a man or a woman in the cold you feel their solid warmth beside you, which is not so apparent in higher temperatures. There is a stark beauty like that of snowflakes falling across pale blue skies, and you want to let that body fall into your own somehow. You do not necessarily desire sex when it snows, but the feeling is pretty close. In the cold, I feel the distance and immediacy of bodies in my vicinity.

With love,
M

My dear world,

None will ever know all the things that have died with those who have been here inhabiting, like us. Sometimes, when I look at someone, I feel an ocean within me trying to seep out, pushing against the taut surface of my skin. I want to expand this invisible shoreline, to flow out of myself. I record the excess of myself, nothing more or less, collect it about myself, the saturation of my being, what is more of me. I wonder if when death comes there is a leakage of this sort, an energy that permeates the earth. When someone dies, what of their many loves and lives? How they can simply leave? I do not think they turn into dreams or find their way as ghosts, but I feel there must be something more. Like how if someone says a word, it becomes a little more a part of her, and it slips into the bloodstream like warm wine, and does something, we know, that which will always remain unknown.

With love,
M

My dear world,

I once heard tell of a tall young man who wore a helmet everywhere he went. He bumped his head so often that he decided it was a necessary precaution. Imagine having to protect the space around your head like that. I think we all strive to be like this young man, wearing our respective helmets, protecting ourselves from the doorways and ceilings of the human life. And when we go to sleep at night, when we are running in open fields, when we are sitting still in high-ceilinged places, we can let the helmets fall to our sides. I did not mean for this to nearly rhyme, but I guess it is not a bad thing, for rhyming can create unity, and walking down the street or through a house with a helmet on one's head will have a sweet and certain beat, like a person is trying and succeeding.

With love,
M

My dear world,

To walk with a crowd, one feels overwhelmed by the union of so many arms and legs and brains moving together as one. It is like the way words come together, a coincidence of feeling meeting ways of doing, a confluence of impulse and sound, music of mind and heart, a dance that welcomes what is and is not, rhythm of voices and unspoken thoughts. The angle of our apartness may be hard and deep, but it can also point to something soft. We all know that in the mornings, especially, there are times when one's mind wanders and sets itself. Maybe all of life, walking in crowds, could be like this. I like to find those who help me breathe easy, when I feel the setting of my heart someplace rested.

With love,
M

My dear world,

Here is a little tale of faith . . . A man once told me that in the future my graduation cap can be sold and I can donate all the money to charity, so I should not throw it away or sell it, as I had been contemplating; rather, I should give it to someone — him, for example — for safekeeping. This man said he would be able to keep it for a good dozen years or so until his expiration, but that he did not want to overestimate things. I do not know if anyone has ever expressed faith in me in such a strange and sweet manner. My graduation cap has little paper cranes on it covered in sparkly nail polish. Maybe, I think, this man is emblematic of all the encouragement I have received, and anything I offer to you, dear world, is the byproduct of a strange love.

With love,
M

My dear world,

I must remind myself of something I told myself to remember, though I do not know if it is true. I tell myself that you told me to go find a rose, to find something out. You told me to be nothing and to practice this by closing my eyes and leaning my body forward and backward so as to avoid occupying the same space too much at once. You were generally insistent that I walk about, outside and in the mind for long periods of time, to love and to be everything and everyone, and so I tried to oblige. I wanted to do right, be right, understand things in their raw forms. To know all that is foreign by instinct. I felt open to and sure of the generosities of life and the phases of it all, like solid little phrases I knew to be poetic. In short, I realized living. I hope I will remember. I am forgetting already.

With love,
M

My dear world,

It is the most difficult thing to ready oneself for recalling the former moment. To look behind at memories, those little flowers, those pink setting suns. There is a comfort to it, of course, but also a deep and abiding sadness for what was beautiful. I wondered what would become of us, little petals packed so close together all those long years, and then a new season came and I knew we must go our separate ways. I hoped we would land softly and find one another in a different form one day. I willed myself into a reverie. I realized I desire only the beautiful, and sometimes the beautiful is not joyful even if it often is. Maybe I realized there is no sure thing — not you, not even my body, definition of lines, aching into itself.

With love,
M

My dear world,

Falling in love with you was unexpected, inevitable. Just as libraries lend urgency to words and death lends gravitas to life, you lend a certain something to my days. I love you so much that sometimes my heart aches. You are wonderful to love. But I am coming to realize that only with time will you see I love you in a way that will stay around for a long while. I think you believe I love you, but it has not been ingrained in your being, as it is in mine. Perhaps, though, you will read these letters — many times — and they will generate time; in other words, they will make moments of us.

With love,
M

My dear world,

I want to see you, but I cannot, and I wonder what you are like and if you want to hold me like I want to hold you. I wonder how whole you are. I wonder if a song can enter you and sink through your body to leap out of your toes. I wonder how much each of us would want to embrace the other despite our misgivings. But I digress. Sometimes it scares me how easily I slip in and out of lives so easily. I leave, I am a leaver. You, gentleness, you. I am hurting you, and I do not want to; I want to be somebody's, to be yours, but I do not exist except in our possibly shared imagination, and you do not either. Or do you? Tell me you exist, please.

With love,
M

My dear world,

My love and I would go on long walks, and I got a sense of what it might be like living life by his side. I felt warm, by him, and would glance at him until he kissed me. I held his arm, and like a gentleman he assisted me across icy sidewalks. Other times he flew across the streets without a care, and I glared at him from behind, wondering what had happened to chivalry. I felt my heart had been roughed up a little when I realized he was not immaculately sweet and that I was not all good. And yet — that he should place one foot outside his world to join mine and that I should do the same was a miracle, and that we should somehow coexist in our various insanities, particularities, was a beautiful thing. I think that is how it must be with you, my dear world.

With love,
M

My dear world,

I suppose folks must fall in love over and over again. I wonder if you, world, are the kind of being a person can fall in love with over and over again and if a person can fall in and out of love with you over the course of their life. I think it would be very tiresome to always love you, world, for I wonder how many shadows humans add to you and how many shadows there are at any given time. I think if you were a word, world, you would be the word *and*. *And* is a word that can bring anything to its unified whole, to completion, and it is one of the humblest words, for it seems always to exist for others rather than itself, and it unifies all that seems irreconcilable, like shadow and light.

With love,
M

My dear world,

The heart can literally ache sometimes when one cries. Once, of many times, there were those tears, and you, perhaps perceiving an aching heart, asked me what I wanted. And it felt like you were opening something of yourself, like you were secretly saying you wanted everything I wanted. But it is hard to say what one wants even when one knows. I care so much, too much. When I care too much, I despair. I want to care less, but it seems an impossibility. To teach myself to passionately care and to live the life of one who is free — that is the question, or one of them at least. I move forward slowly, but it is incorrect still. If you remember, I told you I wanted you, among other things. I wonder why it was so hard to say.

With love,
M

My dear world,

There seems to be a proliferation of sensuality at hand if one would only open one's eyes. Looking at my container of cashews, it occurs to me that they look like pairs of spooning lovers. I wonder if there is any projecting going on and think not, but then I cannot help but see my gala apples, a golden nectarine lying among them, and realize nothing could be more sensual, ripe, round, and possessed of the most fragrant smell. I will only briefly mention the bananas, each lying beside the next so as to slow the ripening process. I am surrounded by raw creation and only barely aware of it. I must open my eyes to the subtleties. I must not seek the sex of a sentence and work on embracing the sensual words surrounding, those that breathe with an ecstasy verging on their arrival.

With love,
M

My dear world,

Sometimes I simply want to touch you. I want to run my fingers along the edges of your clouds, the tips of your fields, the impossible corners of you. For it is nice to feel the edges of things. Edges hint at the possibility of more. An edge resists enveloping. We have the sky and the seas, but you have the stars, everywhere you look. What is it like to feel at once infinitely small and expansive? Maybe it is like moving in a train, when one feels a high, when the trees and bushes and bridges and light pass by in little flashes of ecstasy, so it is like living life over and over again. Like when I see words and cannot bring myself to read them — they resist perusal. One fills one's mind with sky, pictures blue in the mind's eye. There is nothing but you. You are most touchable and untouchable.

With love,
M

My dear world,

The lit underbellies of the leaves beckon. To feel generous, ready, like a child — ! To be reacquainted with sincerity. Maybe beauty is the only thing that has lasting power over me; maybe it is the only lasting thing. I am engaged in making loveliness and spotting the starlight between words and trying to consider what no one else cares for. I cannot help but love what glows. I always trust a naturally glowing thing, like the lit leaves or the moon or the stars. They evoke feeling. I've dreamt so many dreams of feeling, pure and sweet, that honey which keeps the heart so ready.

With love,
M

My dear world,

I cannot help but wonder if this, lying in bed, thinking, a cup of tea by my side, is the best way to end the day. I feel free to think this way, and though my body sinks downward, my heart rests suspended above, gentle and free. I imagine you when you speak, a soft sun on your tongue. I recall your rounded depths. Sometimes I like to miss you because I know we will be together again. To receive what or whom one dearly hopes for — I am lucky in that sense. Yes, I will admit I hope for us. A thought lay close to the bottom of my heart, but I could not hear it — and nothing compelled me to listen for a long while — until I was ignored. The thought was this: that I am addressing a concept of you, but even so, loving you can only be good.

With love,
M

My dear world,

To leave those folk behind, those lit rooms, and you as I knew then — that was difficult. I think the atmosphere of accumulation, of encounters, of all the little objects and lovely people, made for something like timelessness. The clumps of cinnamon in my cider, the cold that could make a person more aware and awakened to all those other lives, the general thereness of things. For a short time, I sold small things that would go away one day, and it was the first time I could claim I was happy, absurdly happy. To experience the instant, life condensed in distinct bits like paper and beads all lined up on a string. The regularity of chaos combined with the immensity of imagination and the shy humility of a moment. It was all about feeling, with a beautiful ache in the breath.

With love,
M

My dear world,

When I rode my bike at midnight with the wind and dark, it was easy to forget about thinking for love of feeling. I would wonder how many others were able to experience the touch of carefree wind. To live in the movement of getting from one point to another, the rush of transience in space, but also the brief stillness, an extended moment. My nose and hands felt the chill, and I blinked my dry eyes. I stared at the road ahead like a baby, except to occasionally veer about potholes or rock my bike back and forth, winding down to a pause. There is nothing quite like breathing in night on my bike, breathing you in. I hope to do it again and again.

With love,
M

My dear world,

Looking down at the city from the sky, the lights look like streets of gold, full of stars. And when the clouds shroud the lights, the city looks its most spectacular, so vaguely there, like a fairyland or residence of ghosts. The horizon is the meeting of two deep blacks. I know that, looking up from earth, the buildings are all alight vertically and horizontally, little magic stacks. I know that the houses look like little colorful pieces of paper stuck together (with stars in between) and the city is like a fresh warm breath and the air is a sunny wet cloud, and the people are like you and me, such people. When I blink, I can hear the squeak of eyeballs in sockets and feel how the nose gets warmer when I come in from the cold. Returning is like this — an adjustment, a fitting of bodies and places and people, and it will never grow old.

With love,
M

$\sim$ VI $\sim$

Your constant arrival

My dear world,

Is life continuously fulfilling itself? I see words and think them to be in a constant state of breath, inhaling and exhaling the space about them. The sky lends a kind of breathless excitement as it pushes itself into the beings of things, and they cannot help but give all of their selves back. Maybe the sky is jealous of the sea because the sea takes the beauty of the sky and makes itself even more beautiful. World, you are transforming. Your light makes everything take on different forms of being. The sun's rays on the river, dusk on a velvet petal, the sky resting on mountain edges — your light paints surfaces, embraces depths. I like when the sky is easy, easy to look at, cloudy or in sunset. At night, in sleep, we need to slip out of this world once in a while, for sleep is a softness purring, where hanging space rests, but the return is always sweet. When the shy sky comes into the morning I am reminded of your constant arrival.

With love,
M

My dear world,

Everything that ever meant anything is accumulating —
at least that is the hope. To write in a state of breath-
lessness, to revel in your presence. I like to nestle into
a thought of you, to look up at city windows when they
are full of sky, to fold each day into a shape. I like to meet
a person and smile in the kind of way that says, "Well,
here we are in the world and look at what it has offered
us." I like to contemplate the tip of a pencil, to think
thoughts such as that there are few things more moving
than a stack of books. I like when the words keep seeping
out like a smile that cannot be helped. I stretch my jaw
and feel more ready to approach you, world. I feel myself
becoming a little odder and a little older as the days go by,
and it is not altogether unpleasant. I am filled to the brim
with words and meanings and find myself grasping onto
the nonfiction of you, your unspoken inner life.

With love,
M

My dear world,

After the rain, the tree seemed to sparkle uncontrollably. It sat, and it quietly grew, and it glistened. The tree made me want to create something that would demand to continue to live. I saw you in that tree. I wanted to fit a galaxy in a sunbeam. I wanted a word or at least to belong to a word. I wanted to put an apple up to my face and smell it, hard and sweet under my nose. I wanted everyone to realize a rose is a kind of lovely onion. I wanted to speak to you of how in some places, the sun is so much brighter, brighter than any place I have been before. I wanted to harness the energy of the inner core of a rose, an onion, the sun. After all these thoughts passed, I knew I was all right because I returned to normal amounts of boredom and daydreaming, but I wonder if you experience such lapses of mind.

With love,
M

My dear world,

I love a big belly. There is nothing effortful about a big belly, at once a slight bump and bulging force. A reminder of the way we fit ourselves into small spaces, the way we unintentionally expand. I like to be squeezed, the lines of me pushed together in a jumble of geometry. I like to send myself out into you, world. I like to send meaning in sound, but space will do it too. Though I am still trying to determine what makes a belly beautiful. Maybe the belly is beautiful because it reminds a person of how desire can fill or leave the body, how a bit of wind can go in and out. The belly seems to be about fulfillment and abatement, a consideration of space. I embrace the belly of you, world.

With love,
M

My dear world,

We so seek to feel alive, to make the most of this life. It seems we are always seeking something joyful even if we do not know it. We wonder if the lovely light of our lives might shatter. Maybe we must exert concentrated focus on the pursuit of wonder. Let us smoke life, let us breathe light, let us fill our beings with sky. Let us use our fingers to pry into the dry cracks of the earth. Let us squeeze the rough bark of fallen trees with our thighs. Let us take our tongues and stick them out and waggle them in the wind. Let us walk, loving, let us walk and love, walking along, loving. Let us seek things that evoke, that suggest something more than themselves. I would like to be an open, questioning being. I would like to become aware of myself — even though you can only stroke a word so much or know a thing so well.

With love,
M

My dear world,

I find myself intrigued by my aging. I await it, breathless, not quite placed. I wait for time to sweep me up like a lover, for things to pass in a daze, to wake up and realize I have met time, and like — love — her. Maybe aging is a matter of falling in love with the passage of time. Maybe one knows one has fully aged when one is ready to be passed by time. It is nice to be the one who is passed by and not to take responsibility for the passing. I rest in the moment and slightly to the side. I use the present tense to indicate to myself my contentedness, my restedness. I live in a secret and solitude that help me recall myself. I do my best thinking while pretending to myself I am reading; I do my best living while pretending to myself I am sleeping. I repeat myself as a reminder to myself of an aspect of who I might be. I age. It is like how missing someone can be one of the sweetest feelings. Maybe that is my relationship to time. Time is a distant lover, always passing by.

With love,
M

My dear world,

How does one know one has reached the ranks of woman?
Perhaps one knows one is a woman when one feels that
the stomach forms the center of one's being, when
wandering about words one gets lost so fast, when one
wonders if it is possible to circumvent impending
heartache, when one has an intuition of her death, when
one decides to develop loyalties to the a-abstract, when
one can feel the morning slipping into the body like a
moonbeam, when one wonders if birthing a baby may
be a way of trying to come home to oneself, when one
grasps for words because one refuses to grasp for any god,
when one wonders if one has unintentionally developed
a philosophy. Perhaps one never really knows anything
at all about being a woman or a man — but for a sense,
hopefully, of some shared humanity.

With love,
M

My dear world,

There is nothing quite like walking in a graveyard. In a graveyard, one feels the presence of bodies shaped like teardrops. One realizes someone in the world needs someone exactly like yourself. One feels almost dispossessed. But then sometimes a breath will feel much nicer after you have not breathed for a long time. One realizes one has come only to leave. Coming to leave. That the day would be gold and blue if you were to take a snapshot of it. In a graveyard, something quiet like perfect solitude brews on the air. One finds one does not need to read the clouds although one can try. One searches for the landscape of the self to try to claim the space around just a little more. You want to be sinking, seeping into the earth, to feel your heart bend a little ways away, like it is beating to another form than blood, and you tell yourself to recall the moment you forgot where you were, that is, when you were displaced, the dirt itself, soft and rough.

With love,
M

My dear world,

Sometimes I want to sing to a field of grass, not just a blade. I want to lick the dew off waxy leaves. I want to pat a belly because a good belly is like a second person: a reassuring, solid presence, an inconspicuous little being. I want to put stamps upside down on my envelopes like my mother. I want to read the speaking shadows. I want to pull on a pair of water wings. I want to sing so much the walls open up. I want to eat an orange so big and beautiful it looks like you, world. I want to sit in a dusty room and tap my shoes, inadvertently causing the dust to rise. I want to speak to words: awake, little word, to the sounds of the world — wren's wandering walk, men and women's trembling hearts, awake to endless dance about the earth. It would seem sometimes that everything is alive.

With love,
M

My dear world,

Maybe love is a lifetime of looking. Curve of his belly ears lips smile arms brows cheeks hands body beautifully alive beside me. A funny furrow in his brow made me frequently want to pronounce love. The edge of a feeling often finds a thought for company. Will I ever be able to love someone in a way that is not tied up in language? Words bring to paper a shape of love. Maybe he occupies the space between thought and silence. Maybe words used to weigh a little more heavy when they traveled on the cost of a stamp. Is there a wasted thought, a wasted breath, a wasted feeling, a wasted word? Is it true that what is beautiful survives? Is a notebook perfect chaos? How heavy is a life? Is repetition an attempt at reassurance? To put one's entire being into loving and simply that — maybe there is no way to love but unconditionally.

With love,
M

My dear world,

You are sweetly obstinate in your ways. There is a wisdom in the words "I once fell in love with a man." Does love creep up on a person or grow under one's nose, or both? Does greater love between two people create a better kind of child? He was a sliver of moon with an edge of sun, like a poem. His feet warmed my bare ones through his shoes. Cold air, last snow, our warmth, a white night pressing us close. Entwined, we slept like babies, covers closing us into each other's arms. I wanted to toss him into gray skies and watch him come tumbling down to me. I considered whether or not he would leave me poemless. I taught myself to breathe about him. I taught myself to be familiar with the varying atmospheres you offer. I fell out of and in love with you all at once.

With love,
M

My dear world,

I am beginning to think that a poet cannot be what might be referred to as a practical person. A poet is most abstract. One can live to death or die to death, and maybe a poet does both. Maybe, even, a poet feels broken when she or he cannot write a poem. I will never be a poet, belong to poetry or prose. I will call myself a putter-togetherer of words and nothing more. I will not feel excited to see a word. I will not allow bookshelves to make me feel at home. I will not think that the most unproductive days are the most productive of all. I will not set up a fund granting poets a certain number of pens per year with the possibility of additional pens upon application if the supply runs out. I will focus on feeling anything but poetic. I will invest in penny stocks instead. I will be a physicist considering time and space. No, I will continue to think you are sweet and proteinaceous, earth, like a salted, roasted almond.

With love,
M

My dear world,

Sometimes you can only write a word because anything else is not enough. Shaping a likeness of myself, I offer it to you, dear world, so that I may keep up with who I am. I familiarize myself with a notion of you and nothing more. I come from a vague place. I am no rose. Go, see for yourself who I am by asking me a question, and I will become uninteresting to you. Please know I grow quiet come autumn. The leaves in the fall seem to be a filter for what I think I know, and that turns out to be only what I feel. And yet I tire of words stitched with space wanting to say something. I consider myself a guilty exception, for you must have realized I like to try to be the leaf, falling, stitching sky, hovering on the edge of the unsaid. Please keep trying to find me, and I will keep seeking you.

With love,
M

My dear world,

I like to stare, for I like to feel the thereness of things, and the eyes want rest. There is always something to embrace with the gaze. My eyes have an affinity for open space and stillness, though others' eyes may rest best in other things. I always hold the tangle of you in my mind's eye. Though I do not always wonder about things as one might suppose. My wondering has limits. There is little contemplation involved. As you know, one of the most difficult things is to be. Familiarizing oneself with oneself is a lifelong project. I hover for you, for myself, for that is one of the ways I know how to live. I am less than you minus the sky and yourself a thousand times. That is to say, I am a void. I am words, languageless, mute but for what I suggest, except perhaps with the lingering presence of my eyes, sometimes.

With love,
M

My dear world,

I am trying to offer myself to you as a kind of love, and I think it's high time you try to do the same — try to be love for a bit, won't you? It's like how one cannot reasonably oppose nudity among animals — I do not oppose the nudity of you, my dear, and I do not suppose you oppose the nudity of me. The best kind of love is the naked kind. You know me better than myself, in all my forms, and this means I need not bother with myself too much — I like that. I can think more of us. Please respond. I must admit I have wondered for a while now — if worlds could make love, what would they create? Your potential is astounding.

With love,
M

My dear world,

When one speaks of where one comes from, one feels compelled to speak of where one hopes to go. I will realize things, I suppose. I will have my philosophically bad moments. Once, a man wondered, standing beside me, why he gets up each morning. Asked me why I got up each morning and requested that I write a story for him and win a prize for it. I like to think I could read the ink of his eyes, but I am no storyteller. Maybe I do not think there is such a thing as a story. This story-man told me that once he approached a woman and asked, "Can I talk to you?" She said yes. I suppose that trying to tell a story is like going out, like this, like loving somebody and asking if they'll love you back. Like trying to answer a question. A lovely and simple and maybe impossible thing.

With love,
M

My dear world,

I am a bundle of yearning, chaos of want contained. It is like the feeling that accumulates when you want to hold someone, or that habit of not finishing sentences once started, creating infinite possibilities of the self, leaving things open to future investigation. It is times like these you wonder if everything needs to be presented as something sculpted. I am so raw. I am not drunk or high — but I could speak out like I am, like I want to embrace you, world, with words and words and words. A word is a word is another word more beautiful because of the former and the next and the circle and sun they create.

With love,
M

My dear world,

You can make it hard to love you. Sometimes I cannot stand the quiet in you. But I think I may have figured out just the right way to love you. Sometimes it is easier to digest thoughts of you than to be with you. It occurs to me that I like to be reminded of you, to look up and realize it is raining as I walk along. I like when the world is wet, for things slide into one another all as one. And so I always find myself ready to love again. I address the poetry in you, and I feel weak with waiting for a response. I try to twist a shape out of what I mean, of my meanings. I am trying to create forms to allow you to approach me, even if approaching is not knowing or caring. We all must find our forms. I want to remain a little indecipherable though I know I am glass.

With love,
M

My dear world,

I have visions of you when I am not with you, am shamefully aware of the texture of your absence. I think: I want so much to be unattached, to be able to live without you. I think: I will never belong to anything or anyone. I turn to thoughts of color, light, space, time. I assign myself to spaces and places. I work in layers of sound and try to shape a home for myself in words. Is it not so presumptuous to write a word? To write a word is to give the word a space all of its own. You build a home for it and hope it can find itself at home among all the other words. Nestled in a new place. I suppose, though, that in new places, we are like babies born over and over again. I think of the snow, falling, drifting upward. Of extending the ephemeral. Spaces follow spaces, burgeoning, and the air smells so sweet. I always will return to you.

With love,
M

My dear world,

They seem to think that being a person in this century is a particularly difficult or easy thing. But maybe it is just as difficult and easy as being a person in previous centuries, albeit in different ways. How much grief do we pass by each day? If gentleness were contagious, what would we be? Can one regret a thought? Can one live in sound, in slant rhymes? Darkness can be disguised in the edges of a body. You know of birds, those lit shadows, shadowy lights, flitting across the sky. We are each of us a bird in a body. In the space between bodies lies a solitude formed by the vibration of differing thoughts. Maybe we need to find something to hang on to, then let it go, slowly, and we will have witnessed beauty. Are trees in a perpetual high? If joy's language was music, I would try to sing, always, and if I could not, I would hum.

With love,
M

NOTES

3: *Perhaps I am just a slip of space to you, world, but that is okay. Here I am, bits of slips of space . . .* Louise Erdrich wrote in *The Antelope Wife,* "Earth and sky touch everywhere and nowhere, like sex between two strangers."

10: *I do not know of a beautiful sentence or a true sentence, the most beautiful, the truest . . .* Ernest Hemingway wrote in *A Moveable Feast,* "All you have to do is write one true sentence. Write the truest sentence that you know."

13: *If one wants to know love for certain, one must behold something that makes one so breathless as to feel strangely intense, concentrated, the self in its final encapsulation . . .* Susan Sontag wrote in her journals, "Loving = the sensation of being in an intense form like pure oxygen (as distinct from air)" (*As Consciousness is Harnessed to Flesh: Journals + Notebooks 1964-1980*).

16: *I surrender to the texts of my head and heart . . .* I first heard the notion of "surrendering to a text" from Carole Maso.

18: *I like the way bodies can slip into one another, maybe because a slip as a garment is ever contradictory, a container yet not . . .* My interpretation of a "slip" as container yet not is influenced by Jacques Derrida's notion of the pharmakon in "Plato's Pharmacy" (*Dissemination*). Derrida writes, "If speech could be purely present, unveiled, naked, offered up in person in its truth, without the detours of a signifier foreign to it, if at the limit an undeferred logos were possible, it would not seduce anyone."

19: *We make such a fuss about being free of others, but maybe we simply need to be free of ourselves — or at least live as if it is possible . . .* In her marvelous *Madness, Rack, and Honey: Collected Lectures*, Mary Ruefle notes, "And that is the landmark in the life of an old artist looking at art: the realization that none of us can ever be free from ourselves."

33: *I will lack style, seeking too much to vaguen or specify myself, when in fact it probably exists in the balance between the two . . .* Samuel Beckett made notes to himself to "vaguen" his writing in his manuscripts. Again, I learned this from the great Carole Maso.

36: *I am glad to report that I have found that a gentle person — with a body fully acquainted with aches and dreams — always comes along . . .* Richard Brautigan wrote, "I have a gentle life," in his splendidly strange *In Watermelon Sugar*.

44: *It was not the Scandinavian couple that would adopt Yao, but an American woman . . .* In 1996, my mother wrote "Recollections of Yao's adoption and since."

87: *Maybe one reads because the text is seductive, just as one's gaze gravitates toward a photograph, figure, or film that sufficiently seduces . . .* During an interview I once conducted with photographer Lucas Foglia, he spoke of his interest in creating seductive photographs.

92: *You do not necessarily desire sex when it snows, but the*

feeling is pretty close . . . This is a reference to Mary
Ruefle's opening prose poem in *The Most of It.*

102: And *is a word that can bring anything to its unified
whole, to completion, and it is one of the humblest words,
for it seems always to exist for others rather than itself,
and it unifies all that seems irreconcilable, like shadow
and light . . .* Mary Ruefle quotes Keats: "[He] said
only one thing was necessary to write good poetry: a
feeling for light and shade. I like that he had the sense
to call it one thing, and not two things" (*Madness, Rack,
and Honey: Collected Lectures*).

119: *Perhaps one knows one is a woman when one decides
to develop loyalties to the a-abstract . . .* In *The Book of
My Lives*, Aleksandar Hemon observes, "Part of growing up is learning, unfortunately, to develop loyalties
to abstractions: the state, the nation, the idea."

128: *I will have my philosophically bad moments . . .* The
phrase "philosophically bad moments" is from
Michael Puett, who kindly allowed me to sit in on a
course of his.

129: *I am not drunk or high — but I could speak out like I
am, like I want to embrace you, world, with words and
words and words . . .* Charles Baudelaire's "Get Yourself
Drunk" and Pablo Neruda's "Poetry" come to mind.

ACKNOWLEDGMENTS

There are many to thank! To those I have known through the paper crane — Anita and Xuemei, Barrett H, Christina G, Diana and Donald, Frankie J, George D, Ginny M, Gregory D, John and Wombi, Mike H, Robert and Kelly, Steve S, and many others who shall go unnamed. To those folks of that complex country which is our world. To Carole and Joanna, for embracing different forms and encouraging my words. To Lindsey Alexander, editor, and Sara Zieve Miller, artist, for great insight, admirable patience, and inspirational aesthetic sensibilities. To Abby, Liz, Randy, Sam, and Sarah, word friends. To Jasmina, Jurica, and Nestor, for being there. To Ken, for making an egg, finding an awl, and believing. To mom, Maggie, there are no words.

ABOUT

Meia Geddes was born in Hefei, China, raised in Sacramento, California, and lives in Boston, Massachusetts.